We hope this book has been informative and helpful on your journey to understanding and celebrating older adults. Thank you for your interest and support!

Title: Travel and Tourism-The Essential Guide to the Capitals' Attractions
Subtitle: A Foodie's Guide to Each Capital: Where to Eat and Drink

Series: Cosmopolitan Chronicles: Tales of the World's Great Cities
By Kelli Tempest

"The world is a book, and those who do not travel read only one page."
Saint Augustine

"A city is not gauged by its length and width, but by the broadness of its vision and the height of its dreams."
Herb Caen

"The purpose of life is to live it, to taste experience to the utmost, to reach out eagerly and without fear for newer and richer experience."
Eleanor Roosevelt

"The only way to do great work is to love what you do."
Steve Jobs

"Travel makes one modest. You see what a tiny place you occupy in the world."
Gustave Flaubert

"Cities were always like people, showing their varying personalities to the traveler. Depending on the city and on the traveler, there might begin a mutual love, or dislike, friendship, or enmity."
Roman Payne

"The best way to predict the future is to create it."
Abraham Lincoln

"The world is a beautiful book, but of little use to him who cannot read it."
Carlo Goldon

"In every walk with nature, one receives far more than he seeks."
John Muir

Table of Contents

Introduction
Purpose of the book

The purpose of this book is to provide an essential travel guide to the capital cities around the world. Whether you are a seasoned traveler or a first-time visitor, this book will offer you an in-depth insight into the must-see attractions, hidden gems, and practical travel information for each capital city.

The book is designed to be a one-stop-shop for anyone who is planning to visit a capital city and wants to make the most of their trip. By offering a comprehensive guide to each city, we hope to inspire and inform readers about the rich history, culture, and experiences that each city has to offer.

The aim of this book is to help travelers to plan their trips more efficiently and effectively, by providing them with all the information they need in one place. We understand that planning a trip can be overwhelming, especially when it comes to choosing what to see and do, where to stay, and how to get around. That is why we have created this guide to simplify the planning process and ensure that travelers have a stress-free and enjoyable experience.

In addition to providing practical travel information, this book also aims to showcase the diversity and uniqueness of each capital city. By highlighting the must-see attractions and hidden gems, readers will gain a deeper appreciation of the local culture and customs, and will be able to explore the city like a local.

Ultimately, the purpose of this book is to inspire readers to travel and explore the world. We believe that travel has the power to broaden our horizons, challenge our perspectives, and create unforgettable memories. By sharing our knowledge and expertise, we hope to encourage readers to step out of their comfort zones and embark on their own travel adventures.

In summary, this book aims to provide a comprehensive guide to the capital cities around the world, highlighting the must-see attractions, hidden gems, and practical travel information. Our goal is to simplify the planning process and inspire readers to explore the world and experience the rich history, culture, and diversity that each capital city has to offer.

Overview of the capital cities covered in the book

In this section, we will provide an overview of the capital cities covered in this book. We have chosen a diverse range of cities from around the world, each with its own unique history, culture, and attractions. From the bustling streets of Tokyo to the historic landmarks of Rome, there is something for every type of traveler in this guide.

Chapter 1: Must-See Attractions

The first chapter of the book will cover the must-see attractions in each of the capital cities. In Tokyo, readers can visit the Imperial Palace, Shibuya Crossing, and the famous Tsukiji Fish Market. In Paris, readers can explore the iconic Eiffel Tower, the Louvre Museum, and the Notre-Dame Cathedral. In New York City, readers can visit the Statue of Liberty, the Empire State Building, and Times Square.

Chapter 2: Hidden Gems

The second chapter of the book will cover the hidden gems in each of the capital cities. In Tokyo, readers can visit the quaint streets of Yanaka, the retro neighborhood of Shimokitazawa, and the peaceful Shinjuku Gyoen National Garden. In Paris, readers can explore the charming Montmartre district, the quirky Catacombs, and the picturesque Buttes-Chaumont Park. In New York City, readers can discover the bohemian vibe of Greenwich Village, the vibrant street art scene in Bushwick, and the peaceful High Line Park.

Chapter 3: Practical Travel Information

The third chapter of the book will provide practical travel information for each of the capital cities. This will include information on transportation, accommodation, dining, and nightlife. Readers will learn how to navigate the public transport systems, find the best places to stay, and discover the local cuisine and nightlife.

Chapter 4: Cultural Experiences

The fourth chapter of the book will cover the cultural experiences in each of the capital cities. Readers will learn about the festivals and events that take place throughout the year, the performing arts and music scene, and the local customs and traditions. From the cherry blossom festivals in Tokyo to the jazz clubs of New Orleans, readers will gain a deeper understanding and appreciation of the local culture.

Chapter 5: Outdoor Activities

The fifth chapter of the book will cover the outdoor activities in each of the capital cities. This will include information on hiking and nature walks, water sports and activities, skiing and winter sports, and adventure tourism. Readers will learn how to explore the natural beauty and outdoor recreation opportunities that each city has to offer.

Chapter 6: Day Trips and Excursions

The sixth chapter of the book will cover the day trips and excursions that readers can take from each of the capital cities. This will include information on nearby towns and villages, national parks and nature reserves, historical and cultural sites, and wineries and vineyards. Readers will learn how to escape the hustle and bustle of the city and discover the surrounding regions.

Chapter 7: Travel Planning and Resources

The final chapter of the book will provide readers with travel planning tips and resources. This will include information on budgeting and cost-saving tips, travel apps and websites, tourist information centers, and travel agencies and tour operators. Readers will learn how to plan their trip effectively and efficiently, and make the most of their time in each of the capital cities.

In summary, this book covers a diverse range of capital cities from around the world, each with its own unique history, culture, and attractions. From must-see landmarks and monuments to hidden gems and outdoor activities, readers will gain a comprehensive understanding of each city and the surrounding regions. Practical travel information, cultural experiences, and travel planning resources are also provided to ensure that readers have a stress-free and enjoyable trip.

Travel tips and advice for readers

In this section, we will provide readers with valuable travel tips and advice to make their trip to the capital cities covered in this book as smooth and enjoyable as possible. We understand that traveling can be stressful, especially when you are in an unfamiliar place, but with the right information and preparation, you can avoid many common travel pitfalls and have an unforgettable experience.

1. Pre-travel planning Before embarking on your journey, there are some things you can do to ensure a stress-free trip. Here are some pre-travel planning tips:

- Make a packing list and check the weather forecast before packing.

- Check the visa and vaccination requirements for the countries you plan to visit.

- Research the local culture and customs to avoid any cultural faux pas.

- Book your accommodation and transportation in advance, especially during peak travel season.

- Purchase travel insurance to protect yourself from unexpected events like flight cancellations or medical emergencies.

2. Transportation Getting around in a new city can be daunting, but with a little preparation, it can be easy and fun. Here are some transportation tips:

- Research the transportation options available in the city, including public transportation, taxis, and ridesharing services.

- Purchase a local transportation pass, if available, to save money on fares.

- Use a GPS navigation app or download offline maps to avoid getting lost.

- If renting a car, make sure you understand local traffic laws and regulations.

3. Safety While the capital cities featured in this book are generally safe for travelers, it is still important to take precautions to ensure your safety. Here are some safety tips:

- Be aware of your surroundings and avoid walking alone in unfamiliar or poorly lit areas.

- Keep your belongings close to you at all times, especially in crowded places like tourist attractions and public transportation.

- Only use licensed taxis or ridesharing services and avoid getting into unmarked vehicles.

- Research any potential scams or tourist traps in advance.

4. Money and budgeting Traveling can be expensive, but with some smart budgeting, you can make your money go further. Here are some money and budgeting tips:

- Research the local currency and exchange rates before your trip.

- Notify your bank and credit card company of your travel plans to avoid any issues with using your cards overseas.

- Look for free or low-cost activities and attractions.

- Consider cooking some of your meals instead of eating out every day.

5. Communication Language barriers can be a challenge when traveling to a foreign country. Here are some communication tips:

- Learn some basic phrases in the local language, such as "hello," "thank you," and "excuse me."

- Use a translation app to help with communication.

- Carry a business card or the address of your accommodation in the local language to show to taxi drivers or locals who can help with directions.

By following these travel tips and advice, you can have a safe and enjoyable trip to the capital cities covered in this book. Remember to be flexible and open to new experiences, and most importantly, have fun!

Chapter 1: Must-See Attractions
Landmarks and monuments

Landmarks and monuments are often the most recognizable and iconic symbols of a city, representing its rich history and cultural significance. In this chapter, we will explore the must-see landmarks and monuments in the capital cities featured in this book, providing readers with an in-depth look at these awe-inspiring attractions.

1. Eiffel Tower - Paris, France The Eiffel Tower is arguably the most famous landmark in Paris and one of the most recognizable structures in the world. Built for the 1889 World's Fair, the tower stands at 324 meters tall and offers breathtaking views of the city from its observation decks. Visitors can also enjoy dining at one of the tower's restaurants or attend a show at the theater located within the tower.

2. Big Ben - London, United Kingdom Located in the heart of London, Big Ben is the nickname for the Great Bell of the clock at the Palace of Westminster. The clock tower stands at over 96 meters tall and is one of the most visited tourist attractions in the city. Visitors can admire the intricate details of the tower's gothic architecture and listen to the famous chimes of the clock.

3. Colosseum - Rome, Italy The Colosseum is one of the most famous landmarks in Rome and one of the largest amphitheaters in the world. Built almost 2,000 years ago, the Colosseum was used for gladiatorial contests and public

spectacles. Today, visitors can tour the structure and learn about its history and significance in Roman culture.

4. Acropolis - Athens, Greece The Acropolis is a complex of ancient ruins located on a hill in Athens, Greece. The most iconic structure within the complex is the Parthenon, a temple dedicated to the goddess Athena. Visitors can tour the ruins and learn about the rich history and mythology of ancient Greece.

5. Great Wall of China - Beijing, China The Great Wall of China is one of the world's most recognizable landmarks, stretching over 13,000 miles across northern China. Built over 2,000 years ago, the wall was designed to protect China from invading armies. Visitors can hike along the wall and take in the stunning views of the surrounding landscape.

6. Taj Mahal - Agra, India The Taj Mahal is one of the most iconic landmarks in India, known for its stunning white marble architecture and intricate details. Built in the 17th century by Emperor Shah Jahan as a memorial to his wife, the Taj Mahal is a UNESCO World Heritage Site and one of the most visited tourist attractions in India.

7. Statue of Liberty - New York City, United States The Statue of Liberty is a symbol of freedom and democracy, gifted to the United States by France in 1886. The statue stands at 93 meters tall and is located on Liberty Island in New York Harbor. Visitors can take a ferry to the island and tour the statue's museum and observation deck.

In conclusion, the landmarks and monuments in the capital cities featured in this book represent the unique cultural and historical significance of each city. From the Eiffel Tower in Paris to the Taj Mahal in Agra, these landmarks are must-see attractions that provide visitors with a deeper understanding and appreciation of the city's rich history and culture.

Museums and galleries

Museums and galleries are some of the most popular attractions in capital cities around the world. They offer visitors a chance to learn about the history, culture, and art of the city and the country. In this chapter, we will explore some of the most fascinating museums and galleries that you should not miss when visiting a capital city.

1. The Louvre Museum, Paris The Louvre Museum is one of the most famous museums in the world. It houses more than 35,000 works of art and artifacts, including the iconic painting of the Mona Lisa. The museum also features collections from ancient Egypt, Greece, and Rome, as well as sculptures, paintings, and decorative arts from the Middle Ages to the 19th century.

2. The British Museum, London The British Museum is one of the oldest museums in the world, with a collection that spans over two million years of human history. Visitors can explore the museum's galleries, which include the Rosetta Stone, the Elgin Marbles, and the Sutton Hoo burial ship, among many other fascinating artifacts.

3. The Smithsonian National Museum of Natural History, Washington D.C. The Smithsonian National Museum of Natural History is home to some of the most fascinating exhibits on natural history in the world. Visitors can explore the museum's vast collections, which include everything from dinosaur fossils to gems and minerals. The museum is also

home to the Hope Diamond, one of the largest and most famous diamonds in the world.

4. The Vatican Museums, Rome The Vatican Museums are home to some of the world's most famous works of art, including the Sistine Chapel and its stunning ceiling painted by Michelangelo. The museums also feature a vast collection of art and artifacts from ancient Egypt, Greece, and Rome, as well as galleries dedicated to modern and contemporary art.

5. The Hermitage Museum, St. Petersburg The Hermitage Museum is one of the largest and most impressive museums in the world, with a collection that spans more than three million works of art and artifacts. Visitors can explore the museum's galleries, which include everything from ancient artifacts to modern art, and marvel at the opulent rooms and halls of the Winter Palace, which houses the museum.

6. The Prado Museum, Madrid The Prado Museum is one of the most important art museums in the world, with a collection that features works by some of the greatest artists in history, including Francisco de Goya, Diego Velázquez, and El Greco. The museum also features collections of sculptures, decorative arts, and prints and drawings.

7. The National Museum of Anthropology, Mexico City The National Museum of Anthropology is one of the most important museums of its kind in the world. It houses a vast collection of artifacts and exhibits related to the pre-Columbian

history and culture of Mexico, including the famous Aztec calendar stone and the Tomb of the Maya King Pakal.

These are just a few of the many museums and galleries that you should not miss when visiting a capital city. Each museum offers a unique and fascinating glimpse into the history, culture, and art of the city and the country. Make sure to plan ahead and book tickets in advance to avoid long lines and ensure you have enough time to explore these incredible institutions.

Parks and gardens

When visiting a capital city, it is important to experience the green spaces and natural beauty that can be found there. In this chapter, we will explore some of the most beautiful parks and gardens in the capital cities featured in this book.

1. Central Park, New York City, USA Central Park is an oasis in the heart of New York City, and a must-visit for any traveler to the city. The park covers 843 acres and is home to many attractions, including the Central Park Zoo, the Central Park Conservatory Garden, and the Central Park Reservoir. Visitors can take a stroll through the park's many paths and admire the beautiful landscaping and architecture. There are also plenty of activities available, such as boating on the lake, picnicking on the Great Lawn, or enjoying a concert at the SummerStage.

2. Tiergarten, Berlin, Germany Located in the heart of Berlin, the Tiergarten is a vast park that covers over 500 acres. Originally a hunting ground for the Prussian royal family, the park is now a popular destination for locals and tourists alike. Visitors can explore the park's many paths and admire the beautiful gardens, fountains, and monuments. The park is also home to many important cultural institutions, such as the Berlin Zoo, the Berlin Philharmonic, and the Haus der Kulturen der Welt.

3. Hyde Park, London, England Hyde Park is one of London's largest and most famous parks, and a must-visit for

any traveler to the city. The park covers 350 acres and is home to many attractions, including the Serpentine Lake, the Diana Memorial Fountain, and the Speakers' Corner. Visitors can take a stroll through the park's many paths and admire the beautiful gardens and monuments. There are also plenty of activities available, such as boating on the lake, horseback riding, or enjoying a concert at the Summer Music Festival.

4. Jardin du Luxembourg, Paris, France The Jardin du Luxembourg is one of Paris's most beautiful and historic parks, and a popular destination for both locals and tourists. The park covers 60 acres and is home to many attractions, including the Luxembourg Palace, the Medici Fountain, and the Orangerie. Visitors can take a stroll through the park's many paths and admire the beautiful gardens and sculptures. There are also plenty of activities available, such as tennis, chess, and pony rides.

5. Ueno Park, Tokyo, Japan Ueno Park is one of Tokyo's most popular parks, and a must-visit for any traveler to the city. The park covers 133 acres and is home to many attractions, including the Ueno Zoo, the Tokyo National Museum, and the Shinobazu Pond. Visitors can take a stroll through the park's many paths and admire the beautiful gardens and temples. There are also plenty of activities available, such as boating on the pond, visiting the nearby Ameya-Yokocho shopping street, or enjoying a concert at the Tokyo Bunka Kaikan.

When visiting these parks and gardens, it is important to follow the rules and respect the natural beauty of the surroundings. Remember to pack sunscreen, a hat, and plenty of water, and be sure to take your trash with you when you leave. With these tips in mind, you can enjoy a peaceful and refreshing break from the hustle and bustle of the city.

Historic districts

A historic district is a section of a city or town that has been designated as historically significant by a local, state, or national authority. These districts are often home to some of the oldest and most architecturally significant buildings and structures in a city, as well as other sites of historical importance. Travelers interested in history, architecture, or simply getting a sense of a city's past will find much to explore in these neighborhoods.

Some of the most famous historic districts in the world are located in major cities like London, Paris, and Rome. However, there are many other lesser-known districts that offer a glimpse into a city's unique history and culture. In this section, we will explore some of the most interesting and significant historic districts around the world.

Old Montreal, Canada

Old Montreal, also known as Vieux-Montreal, is a historic district located in the heart of Montreal, Quebec. The district was founded in the 17th century, and many of its buildings date back to the 18th and 19th centuries. Visitors to Old Montreal can explore narrow cobblestone streets, admire historic architecture, and visit attractions like the Notre-Dame Basilica and the Pointe-à-Callière Museum.

Gamla Stan, Stockholm

Gamla Stan, or "Old Town," is the historic center of Stockholm, Sweden. The district dates back to the 13th century, and its narrow streets and colorful buildings are a popular attraction for tourists. Visitors can explore the Royal Palace, stroll along the waterfront, and enjoy traditional Swedish cuisine in one of the many restaurants and cafes.

French Quarter, New Orleans

The French Quarter is a historic district located in the heart of New Orleans, Louisiana. The district is known for its distinctive architecture, live music, and vibrant nightlife. Visitors can take a walking tour to learn about the area's history, enjoy beignets and cafe au lait at Cafe du Monde, and listen to jazz music at Preservation Hall.

Alfama, Lisbon

Alfama is the oldest district in Lisbon, Portugal, and is known for its winding, narrow streets and colorful buildings. Visitors to Alfama can explore the Castle of Sao Jorge, take a ride on the historic tram, and sample traditional Portuguese cuisine in one of the many restaurants and cafes.

Sultanahmet, Istanbul

Sultanahmet is the historic heart of Istanbul, Turkey, and is home to some of the city's most famous landmarks, including the Blue Mosque, Hagia Sophia, and Topkapi Palace. Visitors to Sultanahmet can explore the area's narrow streets and alleys, enjoy Turkish cuisine in one of the many restaurants, and shop for souvenirs in the Grand Bazaar.

Old Town, Prague

Old Town, or Stare Mesto, is the historic center of Prague, Czech Republic. The district is known for its stunning architecture, including the Old Town Square and the Astronomical Clock. Visitors can also explore the Jewish Quarter, which is home to several historic synagogues and the Jewish Museum.

Historic Charleston, South Carolina

Historic Charleston is a district located in the heart of Charleston, South Carolina, and is known for its well-preserved architecture and Southern charm. Visitors can take a walking tour to learn about the city's history, visit the Battery and Waterfront Park, and sample Lowcountry cuisine in one of the many restaurants and cafes.

Centro Histórico, Mexico City

Centro Histórico, or the Historic Center, is the oldest district in Mexico City and is home to many historic buildings and landmarks, including the Zocalo, the Palacio de Bellas Ar tes, and the Metropolitan Cathedral. The Zocalo is the city's main square and is one of the largest public plazas in the world. It has been a gathering place for people since the Aztec era and continues to be a popular spot for events and celebrations. The Palacio de Bellas Artes is a stunning building that houses a theater and museum, and is known for its impressive Art Nouveau and Art Deco architecture. The Metropolitan Cathedral, located on the north side of the Zocalo, is the largest cathedral in the Americas and took almost 300 years to build. It is an important religious site for Catholics and also an architectural masterpiece.

Aside from these well-known landmarks, the Centro Histórico is full of charming colonial-era buildings and picturesque streets. Walking around the district, visitors will find themselves transported back in time, with the architecture and atmosphere reminiscent of the city's colonial past. One notable building is the Casa de los Azulejos, or House of Tiles, which is covered in blue and white tiles and is a popular spot for photos. Another must-visit attraction is the Templo Mayor, an archaeological site that was once the center of the Aztec empire. Here, visitors can see the ruins of the Aztec pyramids and learn about the fascinating history of the ancient civilization.

In addition to the historical and cultural attractions, the Centro Histórico is also a great place to shop and eat. The district is home to many markets and street vendors selling traditional Mexican crafts and food, as well as high-end boutiques and restaurants. One popular market is the Mercado de San Juan, which is known for its exotic foods and ingredients. There are also many traditional cantinas and cafes where visitors can try local specialties like churros and hot chocolate.

Overall, the Centro Histórico is a must-visit destination for anyone traveling to Mexico City. Its rich history, stunning architecture, and vibrant culture make it a truly unforgettable experience. Whether you're interested in ancient civilizations, colonial architecture, or simply exploring the sights and sounds of a new city, the Centro Histórico has something for everyone.

Chapter 2: Hidden Gems
Local markets and food stalls

One of the best ways to experience a city's culture and cuisine is to explore its local markets and food stalls. Here are some of the must-visit markets and stalls in the capital cities covered in this book.

1. La Boqueria, Barcelona, Spain La Boqueria is a food market located in the heart of Barcelona's Gothic Quarter. It has been in operation since the 13th century and offers a wide variety of fresh produce, seafood, meats, and other local specialties. Visitors can sample delicious tapas, fresh juices, and other snacks at the many food stalls inside the market.

2. Borough Market, London, UK Borough Market is one of the oldest and most famous food markets in London. It is located in Southwark and offers a wide range of gourmet foods from around the world. Visitors can try everything from fresh oysters and cheese to exotic spices and artisanal chocolates.

3. Chatuchak Weekend Market, Bangkok, Thailand Chatuchak Weekend Market is one of the largest markets in the world, with over 15,000 stalls selling everything from clothing and accessories to antiques and handicrafts. Visitors can also sample some of Thailand's famous street food, such as pad thai, grilled meat skewers, and mango sticky rice.

4. Naschmarkt, Vienna, Austria Naschmarkt is Vienna's largest outdoor market and has been in operation since the 16th century. It offers a wide range of local and international foods,

including fresh fruits and vegetables, meats, cheeses, and spices. Visitors can also try some of Austria's famous sweets, such as apple strudel and sachertorte.

5. Grand Bazaar, Istanbul, Turkey The Grand Bazaar is one of the world's oldest and largest covered markets, with over 4,000 shops and stalls selling everything from textiles and jewelry to ceramics and spices. Visitors can also sample traditional Turkish snacks such as baklava and Turkish delight.

Tips for Visiting Local Markets and Food Stalls:

- Go early in the morning to beat the crowds and get the freshest produce.

- Bring cash as many vendors may not accept credit cards.

- Be adventurous and try new foods and flavors.

- Ask vendors for recommendations and tips on how to prepare and cook their products.

- Keep an eye on your belongings and be aware of pickpockets and other scams.

- Follow basic hygiene practices such as washing your hands before and after eating.

Exploring local markets and food stalls is a fun and exciting way to experience a city's culture and cuisine. Make sure to add these markets and stalls to your travel itinerary for a truly authentic experience.

Off-the-beaten-path neighborhoods are those areas that are not frequently visited by tourists but are rich in culture, history, and unique experiences. These neighborhoods often offer an alternative perspective to the mainstream tourist areas, allowing visitors to immerse themselves in the local way of life. In this section, we will explore some of the off-the-beaten-path neighborhoods in the capital cities covered in this book.

1. Prenzlauer Berg, Berlin, Germany Prenzlauer Berg is a neighborhood in the northern part of Berlin known for its charming atmosphere and bohemian vibe. This neighborhood was once a working-class district that underwent gentrification in the 1990s. Today, Prenzlauer Berg is home to many artists, musicians, and young professionals. Visitors to this neighborhood can explore the streets lined with cafes, boutiques, and galleries. One of the must-see attractions in Prenzlauer Berg is the Kulturbrauerei, a former brewery that has been transformed into a cultural center.

2. Gracia, Barcelona, Spain Gracia is a neighborhood in Barcelona that has managed to retain its small-town feel despite being in the heart of the city. This neighborhood is known for its narrow streets, lively squares, and colorful buildings. Visitors to Gracia can explore the local markets, such as Mercat de la Llibertat, which sells fresh produce and other goods. Another must-see attraction in Gracia is the Park Guell, a public park designed by Antoni Gaudi.

3. Montmartre, Paris, France Montmartre is a neighborhood in Paris known for its artistic heritage and stunning views of the city. This neighborhood was once home to many famous artists, including Pablo Picasso and Vincent van Gogh. Visitors to Montmartre can explore the cobblestone streets lined with cafes, galleries, and souvenir shops. One of the must-see attractions in Montmartre is the Sacre-Coeur Basilica, a beautiful church that offers panoramic views of the city.

4. Gamla Stan, Stockholm, Sweden Gamla Stan is the old town of Stockholm and is one of the best-preserved medieval city centers in Europe. This neighborhood is known for its narrow alleys, colorful buildings, and historic landmarks. Visitors to Gamla Stan can explore the Royal Palace, which is the official residence of the Swedish royal family. Another must-see attraction in Gamla Stan is the Stortorget, a beautiful square that is surrounded by historic buildings.

5. Yanaka, Tokyo, Japan Yanaka is a neighborhood in Tokyo known for its traditional Japanese atmosphere and old-fashioned charm. This neighborhood is home to many historic temples and shrines, as well as local shops and eateries. Visitors to Yanaka can explore the streets lined with cherry blossom trees, and take a stroll through the Yanaka Cemetery, which is the final resting place of many famous Japanese figures.

These off-the-beaten-path neighborhoods offer a unique perspective to the capital cities covered in this book. Visitors to these neighborhoods can immerse themselves in the local way of life, and experience the culture and history of these cities in a more authentic way.

I. Introduction A. Explanation of the term "lesser-known attractions" B. Importance of exploring lesser-known attractions

II. Europe A. Barcelona, Spain 1. Park Güell 2. Palau de la Música Catalana 3. Gothic Quarter B. Budapest, Hungary 1. Fisherman's Bastion 2. Memento Park 3. Hospital in the Rock

III. Asia A. Tokyo, Japan 1. Yanaka Ginza 2. Shimokitazawa 3. Tokyo Metropolitan Government Building Observation Deck B. Seoul, South Korea 1. Bukchon Hanok Village 2. Namsan Park 3. Ihwa Mural Village

IV. North America A. Montreal, Canada 1. Parc Jean-Drapeau 2. Plateau Mont-Royal 3. St. Joseph's Oratory B. Austin, Texas, USA 1. Barton Springs Pool 2. Hope Outdoor Gallery 3. Cathedral of Junk

V. South America A. Buenos Aires, Argentina 1. Caminito 2. Palermo Hollywood 3. Tierra Santa B. Montevideo, Uruguay 1. Solís Theatre 2. Prado Park 3. Mercado del Puerto

VI. Oceania A. Melbourne, Australia 1. Hosier Lane 2. St. Kilda Beach 3. Royal Botanic Gardens Victoria B. Auckland, New Zealand 1. Piha Beach 2. Mount Eden 3. Devonport

VII. Conclusion A. Recap of the importance of exploring lesser-known attractions B. Encouragement to readers to discover their own hidden gems during their travels

Note: This outline is not exhaustive and can be adjusted to fit the needs of the book.

Quirky and unique experiences

While visiting a new city, it's always exciting to discover the hidden gems and off-the-beaten-path attractions that are unique to that destination. In this chapter, we'll explore some of the quirky and unconventional experiences that you won't find in your typical travel guide. From bizarre museums to unexpected outdoor activities, these attractions are sure to give you a one-of-a-kind travel experience.

1. Trampoline Parks Trampoline parks are a relatively new type of attraction that have been popping up all over the world. These indoor facilities are filled with interconnected trampolines, foam pits, and other fun features that make for a great workout and an even better time. They're perfect for families, groups of friends, or anyone who wants to try something new and exciting.

2. Secret Bars and Speakeasies If you're looking for a unique night out, consider visiting a secret bar or speakeasy. These hidden gems often require a special password or secret entrance to gain access, and once inside, you'll find a cozy and intimate atmosphere with expertly crafted cocktails and a sense of exclusivity that you won't find in a regular bar. Some of the best secret bars can be found in cities like New York, London, and Tokyo.

3. Underground Tunnels and Catacombs Many cities have a hidden network of tunnels and catacombs that date back centuries. These subterranean attractions can be a fascinating

way to explore a city's history and architecture, but they're not for the claustrophobic. Paris, for example, is famous for its catacombs, which contain the bones of millions of Parisians in a maze of underground tunnels. Meanwhile, Edinburgh's underground vaults offer a spooky and fascinating glimpse into the city's dark past.

4. Street Art Tours If you're a fan of street art, consider taking a guided tour to see some of the best examples of this urban art form. Cities like Berlin, Melbourne, and Buenos Aires are known for their vibrant street art scenes, with murals and graffiti covering buildings and alleys throughout the city. A street art tour will give you a deeper appreciation for this often-overlooked form of public art and introduce you to some talented local artists.

5. Escape Rooms Escape rooms have become increasingly popular in recent years, offering a fun and challenging way to spend an afternoon or evening. These live-action games require you to solve puzzles and clues in order to "escape" from a themed room within a set amount of time. From horror-themed rooms to pirate ship adventures, there's an escape room experience to suit every interest.

6. Unusual Museums If you're tired of the same old art and history museums, consider seeking out some of the more unusual and eclectic museum offerings. For example, Tokyo's Meguro Parasitological Museum is dedicated entirely to parasites, while the Museum of Broken Relationships in

Zagreb, Croatia, explores the stories and emotions behind failed relationships. In the United States, you can visit the International Spy Museum in Washington D.C. or the Museum of Bad Art in Boston for a more offbeat museum experience.

By seeking out these quirky and unique experiences, you'll discover a side of a city that you never knew existed. From trampoline parks to underground tunnels, there's no shortage of unconventional attractions to explore.

Chapter 3: Practical Travel Information
Getting there and around

I. Introduction

- Importance of planning transportation when traveling

- Overview of transportation options for getting to and around capital cities

II. Getting to Capital Cities

- Air travel: Major airports, airlines, and routes

- Train travel: Major railway stations, high-speed trains, and regional trains

- Bus travel: Major bus stations and bus companies

- Car travel: Renting a car and driving in the city

III. Getting Around Capital Cities

- Public transportation: Metro systems, buses, and trams

- Taxis and ride-sharing services

- Bike-sharing and bike rentals

- Walking tours and self-guided walking tours

- Boat tours and water taxis

IV. Tips for Navigating Transportation

- Understanding public transportation systems

- Planning transportation routes in advance

- Purchasing tickets and passes

- Avoiding common transportation scams

V. Special Considerations for Travelers

- Traveling with disabilities

- Traveling with children

- Traveling during peak tourist season

- Navigating language barriers

VI. Conclusion

- Recap of transportation options and tips

- Importance of planning transportation for a successful trip

This content could be expanded or condensed based on the specific capital cities being covered in the book.

Accommodation options

When it comes to planning a trip, one of the most important things to consider is accommodation. Where you choose to stay can greatly impact your overall experience, and there are a wide variety of options available to suit different needs and budgets. In this chapter, we will explore some of the most popular accommodation options for travelers, as well as some unique and interesting options that you may not have considered.

Hotels: Hotels are one of the most common types of accommodation for travelers, and they come in a wide range of styles and price points. From budget-friendly chain hotels to luxury resorts, there are options to suit every traveler. Many hotels offer amenities such as room service, fitness centers, and swimming pools, making them a popular choice for those who want a comfortable and convenient place to stay.

Hostels: Hostels are a popular option for budget-conscious travelers, particularly those who are traveling alone or in small groups. These accommodations typically offer shared dorm-style rooms, as well as private rooms at a lower cost than a traditional hotel. Hostels often have a more social atmosphere, with communal spaces for cooking, eating, and socializing, making them a great option for solo travelers who want to meet new people.

Vacation Rentals: Vacation rentals are a great option for travelers who want more space and privacy than a hotel or hostel can offer. These accommodations can range from private rooms in a shared apartment to entire houses or villas. Vacation rentals are often fully furnished and equipped with amenities such as a kitchen and laundry facilities, which can be particularly appealing for longer stays or for those traveling with a family or group.

Camping: For those who enjoy the outdoors, camping can be a great option for accommodation. There are a wide variety of campsites available, from basic sites with no amenities to full-service campgrounds with electricity, showers, and even swimming pools. Camping can be a particularly affordable option for travelers who have their own equipment, but many campsites also offer rentals for those who don't.

Unique Accommodation Options: For those who want a truly unique and memorable experience, there are a wide variety of unusual accommodation options available. These can range from treehouses and yurts to converted train cars and lighthouses. While these options may be more expensive than traditional accommodation, they offer a one-of-a-kind experience that can make your trip truly unforgettable.

Overall, when choosing your accommodation, it is important to consider your budget, travel style, and the location of your destination. With so many options available, there is something for everyone, whether you are looking for a budget-friendly hostel or a luxurious resort.

Dining and nightlife

When traveling to a new city, exploring the local cuisine and nightlife scene can be just as important as visiting the top attractions. In this section, we will explore some of the best dining and nightlife options in the capital cities featured in this book.

Dining: Every city has its unique food culture, and sampling local dishes is a must for any traveler. In this section, we will highlight some of the best dining options, including restaurants, street food, and markets, in each of the capital cities.

Restaurants: From Michelin-starred fine dining establishments to trendy cafes and bistros, there is no shortage of restaurants to choose from in the capital cities. We will recommend some of the best places to try local specialties, as well as international cuisine.

Street food: Many cities have a vibrant street food scene, where vendors sell delicious and affordable snacks and meals. We will explore some of the best street food markets and stalls in each city, from the traditional to the trendy.

Markets: Local markets can be a great place to sample fresh produce, artisanal products, and street food. We will recommend some of the best markets to visit in each city, where visitors can immerse themselves in the local food culture.

Nightlife: When the sun goes down, many capital cities come to life with a buzzing nightlife scene. From pubs and bars to nightclubs and music venues, there is something for everyone in these cities. In this section, we will highlight some of the best places to experience the nightlife in each capital city.

Pubs and bars: Whether you're looking for a cozy pub to enjoy a pint or a trendy cocktail bar, there are plenty of options to choose from in the capital cities. We will recommend some of the best places to enjoy a drink and soak up the local atmosphere.

Nightclubs: For those who want to dance the night away, many of these cities have world-renowned nightclubs and music venues. We will recommend some of the best places to experience the nightlife, from underground clubs to high-end venues.

Live music: Many of these cities have a vibrant live music scene, with venues ranging from intimate jazz clubs to large concert halls. We will highlight some of the best places to catch a live performance in each city, including local and international acts.

In this section, we will also provide practical information such as opening hours, dress codes, and reservation policies for the recommended dining and nightlife spots.

When traveling to a new destination, it's important to take certain precautions to ensure your safety. While many places are generally safe, it's always a good idea to be prepared and informed before embarking on your trip. This section of the book will provide practical safety tips and advice for travelers to help them stay safe and enjoy their trip.

1. Research the destination: Before you leave for your trip, it's important to do your research on the destination. This includes researching the local customs, laws, and potential safety risks. You can find information on the internet, travel guidebooks, or by asking the hotel staff or locals. By being informed, you can better prepare for potential safety risks and avoid dangerous situations.

2. Stay alert and aware of your surroundings: When you're out and about, always be aware of your surroundings. This means staying alert and paying attention to your surroundings. Avoid walking alone in dark or deserted areas and always keep your belongings close to you. When you're in crowded areas, keep an eye out for pickpockets and keep your valuables secure.

3. Keep important documents and valuables safe: When traveling, it's important to keep your important documents and valuables safe. This includes your passport, ID, credit cards, and cash. Keep them in a secure place, like a hotel safe or a

money belt. Avoid carrying large amounts of cash and only take what you need for the day.

4. Use reputable transportation: When using transportation, like taxis or public transport, make sure to use reputable providers. Research taxi companies or public transport options before you arrive at your destination. This will help you avoid scams and dangerous situations.

5. Avoid unsafe activities: When you're traveling, it's important to avoid activities that could put you in danger. This includes activities like walking alone at night, accepting drinks from strangers, or going to unlicensed establishments. Always use common sense and trust your instincts.

6. Learn basic phrases in the local language: Learning basic phrases in the local language can help you communicate with locals and get help in case of an emergency. Basic phrases like "help" and "where is the hospital?" can be lifesaving in emergency situations.

7. Purchase travel insurance: Finally, consider purchasing travel insurance before you leave for your trip. This can provide you with financial protection in case of an emergency, like a medical emergency or lost luggage.

In conclusion, traveling can be a rewarding and enjoyable experience, but it's important to take precautions to ensure your safety. By following these practical safety tips and advice, you can have a safe and enjoyable trip.

Chapter 4: Cultural Experiences
Festivals and events

One of the best ways to experience the culture of a city is to attend its festivals and events. Whether it's a religious celebration, a music festival, or a food fair, these events provide a glimpse into the traditions, customs, and lifestyle of the locals. In this chapter, we will explore some of the most popular festivals and events in the capital cities covered in this book.

1. Rio Carnival, Brazil Rio de Janeiro's Carnival is one of the world's most famous and vibrant celebrations. Held annually before Lent, the carnival is a four-day extravaganza of parades, samba dancing, and street parties. Tourists and locals alike dress up in colorful costumes and dance to the sound of live music. The highlight of the festival is the Sambadrome parade, where samba schools compete for the title of the best performance.

2. Songkran, Thailand Songkran, also known as the Thai New Year, is celebrated in mid-April with water fights, temple visits, and traditional ceremonies. During this three-day festival, locals pour water over each other to symbolize the washing away of sins and bad luck. The festival is celebrated across the country, but the best place to experience it is in Chiang Mai, where the festivities last for a week.

3. Day of the Dead, Mexico The Day of the Dead, or Dia de los Muertos, is a unique Mexican holiday that honors deceased loved ones. The festival is celebrated on November 1st

and 2nd with parades, offerings, and traditional food. In Mexico City, the festival takes place at the Zocalo, the city's main square, where altars are set up to honor the dead. Visitors can also join in the parade or visit the local cemeteries, where families gather to celebrate the lives of their ancestors.

4. La Tomatina, Spain La Tomatina is an annual tomato fight that takes place in the town of Buñol, near Valencia. Held on the last Wednesday of August, the festival involves thousands of people throwing tomatoes at each other in the streets. The festival started in 1945 as a small street fight and has since become a major tourist attraction.

5. Holi, India Holi is a Hindu festival that celebrates the victory of good over evil and the arrival of spring. Celebrated in March, the festival is known for its colorful powder, which participants throw at each other. The festival is celebrated across India, but the best place to experience it is in the cities of Mathura and Vrindavan, where the festival lasts for a week and includes traditional ceremonies and music.

6. Edinburgh Fringe Festival, Scotland The Edinburgh Fringe Festival is the world's largest arts festival, with thousands of performers and shows taking place over three weeks in August. The festival includes theater, comedy, dance, and music, with performances held in venues across the city. The festival also includes street performers and free events, making it a great way to experience the culture of Edinburgh.

7. Cherry Blossom Festival, Japan The Cherry Blossom Festival, or Hanami, is a Japanese tradition that celebrates the arrival of spring and the blooming of cherry blossoms. The festival is celebrated across the country, but the best place to experience it is in Tokyo, where the cherry blossoms in Ueno Park and Shinjuku Gyoen National Garden draw large crowds. Visitors can enjoy traditional Japanese food and drinks under the cherry blossoms and participate in cultural events.

Conclusion Attending festivals and events is a great way to immerse yourself in the culture of a city and experience its traditions and customs. The festivals and events mentioned in this book are just a small selection of the many cultural experiences that are available in each city. From music festivals to religious celebrations, there are numerous events that take place throughout the year that visitors can attend and enjoy. By participating in these events, travelers can gain a deeper understanding and appreciation of the local culture and its people.

In addition to festivals and events, there are many other cultural experiences that can be enjoyed in the cities featured in this book. These can include attending theater performances, visiting art galleries and museums, trying local cuisine, and exploring historic sites. Each city has its own unique cultural offerings, and by taking the time to explore them, travelers can broaden their horizons and create lasting memories.

Overall, this book aims to inspire and guide travelers as they explore the vibrant and diverse capital cities of the world. From must-see attractions to hidden gems and cultural experiences, each chapter offers a wealth of information and advice to help readers plan their trip and make the most of their time in each city. By following the tips and suggestions in this book, travelers can discover new and exciting destinations, meet new people, and create unforgettable experiences that will stay with them for years to come.

Performing arts and music

One of the most thrilling aspects of traveling to a new city is the opportunity to experience local music and performing arts. From classical concerts to underground music scenes, each city has its own unique offerings that can provide visitors with a truly unforgettable cultural experience.

Classical Music

Many capital cities around the world are known for their classical music scenes, with renowned orchestras and opera houses hosting world-class performances year-round. In Vienna, for example, visitors can attend a concert at the legendary Musikverein or State Opera House, where they will be surrounded by stunning architecture and performances by some of the world's most talented musicians. Similarly, in Moscow, the Bolshoi Theatre is a must-visit destination for classical music and ballet enthusiasts, with stunning productions of timeless classics like Swan Lake and The Nutcracker.

Popular Music

For those who prefer more contemporary genres, many capital cities are also known for their thriving popular music scenes. From intimate jazz clubs in Paris to sprawling dance clubs in Tokyo, visitors can find a diverse array of live music performances to suit any taste. In London, venues like the O2 Arena and Brixton Academy regularly host concerts by some of the world's most popular musicians, while the city's smaller venues like the Roundhouse and the Jazz Café offer visitors a chance to discover emerging artists and up-and-coming talent.

Theater

Theater is also an important part of many capital cities' cultural scenes, with world-renowned productions often originating in cities like New York, London, and Paris. Broadway shows like Hamilton and The Lion King draw visitors from all over the world to New York City, while the West End in London is home to long-running productions like Les Misérables and The Phantom of the Opera. In Paris, the Théâtre de l'Atelier and Théâtre de la Huchette offer visitors a chance to experience cutting-edge theater productions in the heart of the city.

Festivals

In addition to year-round performances, many cities also host music and performing arts festivals that offer visitors a chance to experience a wide range of cultural events in a single location. The Edinburgh Festival Fringe, for example, is the world's largest arts festival, with thousands of performances taking place each August across the city's theaters, bars, and outdoor spaces. Similarly, in Austin, Texas, the South by Southwest festival brings together musicians, filmmakers, and tech innovators for a weeklong celebration of creativity and innovation.

In conclusion, experiencing the performing arts and music scenes in a city can provide visitors with a deeper appreciation for its culture and traditions. From classical music to contemporary dance, there is something for everyone to enjoy, and festivals and events offer visitors a chance to see a wide variety of performances in a single trip.

Cultural institutions

One of the best ways to gain insight into the culture of a city is to visit its cultural institutions. These institutions can include everything from museums and galleries to historical landmarks and cultural centers. In this section, we will explore some of the top cultural institutions in the capital cities covered in this book.

1. National Museum of History and Art, Luxembourg City

The National Museum of History and Art in Luxembourg City is a must-visit for anyone interested in the country's rich history and cultural heritage. The museum's extensive collection includes artifacts and works of art from the Gallo-Roman period to the present day, with a particular emphasis on Luxembourgish history and culture. Highlights of the museum's collection include the ancient Roman mosaic floors from the Villa Echternach, medieval sculptures, and a stunning array of 18th-century French porcelain.

2. Royal Museums of Fine Arts of Belgium, Brussels

The Royal Museums of Fine Arts of Belgium in Brussels is one of the most important art museums in Europe, with a collection of over 20,000 works spanning the medieval period to the present day. The museum's collection includes paintings, sculptures, and decorative arts, with particular emphasis on Belgian artists such as Pieter Bruegel the Elder, James Ensor, and René Magritte. The museum also houses an impressive collection of 19th-century Belgian art, including works by the renowned Realist painter Constantin Meunier.

3. Van Gogh Museum, Amsterdam

The Van Gogh Museum in Amsterdam is home to the largest collection of Vincent van Gogh's works in the world, with over 200 paintings, 500 drawings, and 700 letters. The museum's collection includes some of van Gogh's most famous works, including "The Potato Eaters," "Sunflowers," and "The Bedroom." The museum also features works by other artists who influenced van Gogh, as well as temporary exhibitions that explore different aspects of his life and work.

4. Museum Island, Berlin

Museum Island in Berlin is home to five world-renowned museums, each of which showcases a different aspect of the city's cultural heritage. The Pergamon Museum houses one of the world's largest collections of ancient artifacts, including the famous Ishtar Gate of Babylon. The Neues Museum is home to the iconic bust of Queen Nefertiti, as well as an extensive collection of ancient Egyptian art. The Alte Nationalgalerie features works by German Romantic painters, while the Bode Museum showcases a collection of Byzantine and medieval art. Finally, the Altes Museum houses an extensive collection of Greek and Roman art.

5. Hermitage Amsterdam, Amsterdam

The Hermitage Amsterdam is a satellite of the world-famous Hermitage Museum in St. Petersburg, Russia, and features temporary exhibitions that explore different aspects of Russian art and culture. Recent exhibitions have included "Jewels! Glittering at the Russian Court," which showcased the stunning jewelry collection of the Romanov dynasty, and "Dutch Masters from the Hermitage," which featured works by Dutch artists from the Golden Age.

In conclusion, visiting cultural institutions is an excellent way to gain a deeper understanding of a city's history, art, and culture. The institutions highlighted in this section are just a small selection of the many world-class museums, galleries, and cultural centers that can be found in the capital cities covered in this book. Whether you're interested in ancient history, modern art, or contemporary culture, there is sure to be something to suit your interests in these vibrant and diverse cities.

Local customs and traditions

When traveling to a new city, it's important to be aware of the local customs and traditions in order to have a respectful and enjoyable experience. In this chapter, we'll explore some of the customs and traditions that are unique to each of the capital cities covered in this book.

Paris: Parisians are known for their chic and elegant sense of style, and it's important to dress appropriately when visiting the city. Avoid wearing sneakers, sweatpants, or athletic wear, as these are typically reserved for the gym. When dining out, it's also important to be aware of French dining etiquette, such as keeping your hands on the table and not resting your elbows on it, and waiting for everyone to be served before beginning to eat.

Tokyo: Japan is known for its strict adherence to social etiquette, and it's important to be aware of the customs and protocols when visiting Tokyo. When entering someone's home, it's customary to remove your shoes and place them in a designated area. It's also considered rude to talk loudly in public or to eat while walking.

Rome: Italy is a country with a rich cultural heritage, and the customs and traditions of Rome reflect this history. When visiting religious sites, such as the Vatican or the Pantheon, it's important to dress modestly and respectfully. In general, Italians are very social people and enjoy spending time with friends and family, often over a leisurely meal that can last for hours.

London: As one of the world's most diverse cities, London has a wide range of cultural traditions and customs. When visiting London, it's important to be aware of the local etiquette when using public transportation, such as standing on the right side of the escalator to allow others to pass on the left. Londoners are also known for their dry sense of humor and love of tea, so be sure to indulge in a proper British tea time during your visit.

Madrid: Spain is a country with a strong sense of regional identity, and Madrid is no exception. When visiting the city, be sure to try some of the traditional foods, such as paella or churros con chocolate. In terms of customs, the Spanish are known for their relaxed approach to time, so don't be surprised if meetings or appointments start a bit later than scheduled.

Each of these cities has its own unique customs and traditions, and taking the time to learn about and appreciate them can greatly enhance your travel experience. By being respectful of local customs and traditions, you can gain a deeper understanding and appreciation of the city and its people.

Chapter 5: Outdoor Activities
Hiking and nature walks

Hiking and nature walks are popular outdoor activities that allow travelers to immerse themselves in the natural beauty of a destination. Whether it's a leisurely stroll or a challenging hike, exploring the great outdoors is a great way to stay active and discover new sights.

One of the best things about hiking is that it can be done in many different types of terrain. Some cities have dedicated hiking trails, while others offer opportunities to explore nearby mountains, forests, or national parks. Hiking trails can range from easy to difficult, so it's important to choose a trail that matches your fitness level and experience.

One popular destination for hiking is the Pacific Northwest in the United States. The region is home to some of the most beautiful hiking trails in the world, including the Pacific Crest Trail, which runs from Mexico to Canada. Other popular hiking destinations include the Rocky Mountains, the Swiss Alps, and the Andes.

Nature walks, on the other hand, are typically shorter and more leisurely than hiking trails. They allow travelers to enjoy the natural surroundings at a slower pace, taking in the scenery and spotting local wildlife. Many parks and botanical gardens offer guided nature walks led by experienced naturalists, who can provide insight into the local flora and fauna.

Some popular destinations for nature walks include Central Park in New York City, the Royal Botanic Gardens in London, and the Singapore Botanic Gardens. Many national parks, such as Yellowstone and Yosemite in the United States, also offer nature walks led by park rangers.

No matter where you go, it's important to come prepared for hiking and nature walks. Wear comfortable shoes and appropriate clothing for the weather, bring plenty of water and snacks, and always follow park rules and safety guidelines. With a little planning, hiking and nature walks can be an enjoyable and memorable way to experience the great outdoors.

Water sports and activities

When it comes to outdoor activities, water sports and activities are a popular choice for many travelers. Whether you're looking for a relaxing day on the water or an adrenaline-pumping adventure, there are plenty of options to choose from.

1. Swimming: One of the most popular water activities is swimming. Many destinations offer beautiful beaches or swimming pools for tourists to take a dip in. Just make sure to follow any safety guidelines and be aware of any potential hazards.

2. Snorkeling: If you're looking to explore underwater without the need for scuba gear, snorkeling is a great option. Many beaches and resorts offer snorkeling equipment rentals, and you can see an array of fish, corals, and other marine life.

3. Scuba diving: For those who want to take their underwater exploration to the next level, scuba diving is a must-try activity. There are many locations around the world that are popular for scuba diving, such as the Great Barrier Reef in Australia or the cenotes in Mexico.

4. Surfing: Surfing is a popular water sport that requires balance, strength, and a love for adventure. Many beach destinations around the world offer surfing lessons for beginners, while more experienced surfers can seek out challenging waves and breaks.

5. Stand-up paddleboarding: Stand-up paddleboarding, or SUP, is a fun and relaxing activity that can be done on calm

waters such as lakes, rivers, or the ocean. It's a great way to enjoy nature while getting a workout in.

6. Kayaking and canoeing: Another way to enjoy the water is by kayaking or canoeing. This activity can be done on calm lakes or rivers, or for more adventurous travelers, on rapids or white water.

7. Jet skiing: For those seeking a bit more speed and excitement, jet skiing is a thrilling option. Many beaches or lakes offer jet ski rentals, and it's a great way to explore the area from a different perspective.

8. Parasailing: Parasailing is a popular activity for those who want to see a destination from a bird's-eye view. You'll be strapped into a harness and lifted into the air by a parasail attached to a speedboat.

9. Fishing: If you're looking for a more relaxed activity on the water, fishing is a great option. Many locations offer guided fishing tours or boat rentals, where you can try your hand at catching a variety of fish.

10. Sailing: For those who want to explore the open waters at a leisurely pace, sailing is a wonderful option. You can charter a sailboat or join a group tour, and enjoy the beauty of the ocean while feeling the wind in your hair.

No matter what type of water activity you choose, make sure to follow any safety guidelines and respect the environment you're in. Water sports and activities can be a fun and memorable part of any travel experience.

Skiing and winter sports

Skiing and winter sports are popular activities in many destinations around the world, offering opportunities for adventure, adrenaline, and stunning natural scenery. Whether you're a seasoned skier or snowboarder or a beginner looking to try something new, there are plenty of options for winter sports enthusiasts.

Skiing is the most popular winter sport and can be enjoyed in many countries around the world. The most famous ski resorts are located in the Alps, with popular destinations including Chamonix in France, St. Moritz in Switzerland, and Cortina d'Ampezzo in Italy. These resorts offer a range of slopes suitable for different skill levels, from easy beginner runs to challenging black diamond runs for expert skiers. Many resorts also offer opportunities for off-piste skiing and heli-skiing for those looking for a more adventurous experience.

Snowboarding is also a popular winter sport and is similar to skiing in terms of technique but with a different style and equipment. Many ski resorts offer snowboarding lessons and have designated areas for snowboarders. Popular snowboarding destinations include Whistler Blackcomb in Canada, Park City in Utah, and Hakuba in Japan.

Cross-country skiing, also known as Nordic skiing, is another popular winter sport that involves skiing on flatter terrain than downhill skiing. It can be enjoyed in many destinations, including Scandinavia, Canada, and the United

States. Cross-country skiing is a great way to explore natural scenery and is also a good cardiovascular workout.

Ice skating is another winter activity that can be enjoyed by all ages and skill levels. Outdoor ice skating rinks are popular in many cities around the world during the winter months, and indoor rinks offer year-round ice skating opportunities. Many rinks also offer ice skating lessons for beginners.

Other winter sports include snowshoeing, which involves walking through snow with special shoes that distribute your weight evenly, and ice climbing, which involves using specialized equipment to climb ice formations. Both of these activities offer a unique and challenging way to experience the winter landscape.

When planning a winter sports trip, it's important to pack appropriate clothing and equipment, including warm layers, waterproof outerwear, and specialized gear for your chosen activity. Many ski resorts offer equipment rentals, so you don't have to bring your own gear. It's also important to consider the weather conditions and check the local forecast before heading out to ensure a safe and enjoyable experience.

In conclusion, skiing and winter sports offer an exciting way to experience the outdoors during the colder months. Whether you prefer downhill skiing, snowboarding, or cross-country skiing, there are plenty of destinations and activities to suit all skill levels and interests. So, grab your skis or snowboard and hit the slopes for an unforgettable winter adventure.

Adventure tourism

Adventure tourism is a type of tourism that involves exploring and experiencing the natural and cultural attractions of a destination in an adventurous way. It is perfect for those who are looking for a thrilling and unique travel experience. In this chapter, we will explore some of the most popular adventure tourism activities that you can enjoy during your travels.

1. Zip-lining

Zip-lining is an exciting and thrilling adventure sport that involves sliding down a cable at high speeds while suspended in the air. It is a great way to experience the beauty of a destination from a new perspective while getting your adrenaline pumping. Some of the best places to go zip-lining include Costa Rica, Puerto Rico, and Hawaii.

2. Bungee jumping

Bungee jumping is a popular adventure sport that involves jumping off a high platform while attached to a bungee cord. It is an intense experience that provides an adrenaline rush like no other. Some of the most popular bungee jumping locations include New Zealand, South Africa, and Switzerland.

3. White-water rafting

White-water rafting is an exhilarating adventure activity that involves navigating through rapids and turbulent water in a raft. It is a great way to explore the natural beauty of a destination while experiencing the thrill of the ride. Some of the best places to go white-water rafting include the Grand Canyon, Colorado River, and Zambezi River.

4. Rock climbing

Rock climbing is a challenging and exciting adventure sport that involves climbing up steep rock formations using specialized equipment. It is a great way to test your physical and mental limits while enjoying the beauty of nature. Some of the most popular rock climbing destinations include Yosemite National Park, Joshua Tree National Park, and Red River Gorge.

5. Scuba diving

Scuba diving is an adventure sport that involves exploring the underwater world while wearing scuba gear. It is a great way to experience the beauty of marine life and coral reefs up close. Some of the best scuba diving destinations include the Great Barrier Reef, Belize, and the Maldives.

6. Skydiving

Skydiving is an extreme adventure sport that involves jumping out of an airplane while wearing a parachute. It is a thrilling experience that provides a bird's-eye view of a destination while free-falling through the air. Some of the most popular skydiving locations include Dubai, Hawaii, and California.

7. Heli-skiing

Heli-skiing is a type of skiing that involves being dropped off by helicopter at the top of a mountain and skiing down remote and untouched terrain. It is a unique and exciting way to experience the beauty of a destination's natural environment while enjoying the thrill of skiing. Some of the best heli-skiing destinations include Alaska, Canada, and New Zealand.

8. Caving

Caving is an adventurous activity that involves exploring caves and underground formations. It is a great way to experience the hidden natural beauty of a destination while learning about the geological formations and underground ecosystems. Some of the best caving destinations include Mammoth Cave National Park, Carlsbad Caverns National Park, and Waitomo Caves.

9. Wildlife safaris

Wildlife safaris are a popular adventure activity that involves exploring the natural habitats of wild animals while in a vehicle or on foot. It is a great way to experience the beauty of a destination's natural environment while learning about the local wildlife. Some of the best wildlife safari destinations include South Africa, Tanzania, and Kenya.

In conclusion, adventure tourism offers a unique and exciting way to experience the beauty of a destination while getting your adrenaline pumping. From zip-lining to wildlife safaris, there are many different adventure activities to choose from depending on your interests and level of physical fitness. So, pack your bags and get ready for the adventure of a lifetime.

However, it is important to keep in mind that adventure tourism comes with certain risks and it is essential to choose reputable companies and guides who prioritize safety. Before embarking on any adventure activity, make sure to thoroughly research the company and the activity itself. It is also important to follow all safety guidelines and listen to your guide's instructions. With proper planning and precautions, adventure tourism can be a safe and exhilarating way to experience the great outdoors. So, if you're looking for a thrilling and unforgettable experience, consider adding adventure tourism to your travel itinerary.

Chapter 6: Day Trips and Excursions

Nearby towns and villages

Exploring nearby towns and villages is a great way to get a taste of the local culture and history. Here are some of the best nearby towns and villages to visit during your travels:

1. Sintra, Portugal: Located just 30 minutes outside of Lisbon, Sintra is a UNESCO World Heritage site known for its stunning palaces and castles, including the famous Pena Palace. The town also offers beautiful hiking trails and gardens to explore.

2. Bruges, Belgium: Often referred to as the "Venice of the North," Bruges is a charming medieval town known for its winding canals and historic architecture. Visitors can explore the town on foot or by boat, and indulge in local Belgian cuisine and beer.

3. Bath, England: Home to some of the best-preserved Roman baths in the world, the city of Bath offers visitors a glimpse into the history of ancient Roman civilization. The town is also known for its Georgian architecture and quaint tea rooms.

4. Giverny, France: This small village is famous for being the home of impressionist painter Claude Monet, and visitors can tour his beautiful gardens and home. The town also offers charming cafes and shops, and is just a short train ride from Paris.

5. Cinque Terre, Italy: These five small fishing villages on the coast of Italy offer stunning views of the Mediterranean Sea and colorful architecture. Visitors can hike between the towns or take a train, and enjoy fresh seafood and local wine.

6. Hallstatt, Austria: Nestled in the Austrian Alps, the picturesque town of Hallstatt is known for its stunning mountain views and historic salt mines. Visitors can also explore the town's ancient cemetery and take a boat ride on the Hallstatt lake.

7. Ronda, Spain: Located in the Andalusian region of Spain, Ronda is a historic town perched on a cliff above a dramatic gorge. Visitors can explore the town's ancient bridges and bullfighting ring, and indulge in local tapas and wine.

8. Giethoorn, Netherlands: This quaint village is often referred to as the "Venice of the North" due to its many canals and bridges. Visitors can explore the town by boat or on foot, and enjoy local Dutch treats like stroopwafels and cheese.

9. Zermatt, Switzerland: Located at the foot of the famous Matterhorn mountain, Zermatt is a charming alpine village known for its skiing and outdoor activities. Visitors can also enjoy local Swiss cuisine and explore the town's historic church.

10. Oia, Greece: Located on the island of Santorini, Oia is a picturesque town known for its white-washed buildings and stunning sunsets. Visitors can explore the town's many shops

and restaurants, and take in the beautiful views of the Aegean Sea.

In conclusion, nearby towns and villages offer a unique opportunity to experience the local culture and history of a destination. Whether you're looking for charming medieval towns or stunning mountain views, there's a nearby town or village that's sure to captivate you.

National parks and nature reserves

Introduction: If you're an outdoor enthusiast or nature lover, visiting national parks and nature reserves is an ideal way to spend a day trip or excursion. These protected areas are home to diverse ecosystems, wildlife, and landscapes that offer visitors an opportunity to immerse themselves in nature and experience its raw beauty. This chapter will explore some of the most spectacular national parks and nature reserves around the world and what makes them unique.

1. Yellowstone National Park: Yellowstone National Park is one of the most popular and well-known national parks in the United States. Located primarily in Wyoming, the park spans over 2 million acres and features a diverse range of landscapes, including mountains, forests, and geothermal features. The park is also home to a variety of wildlife, such as grizzly bears, wolves, and elk, making it an ideal destination for wildlife enthusiasts. Some of the top attractions in Yellowstone National Park include the Old Faithful geyser, the Grand Prismatic Spring, and the Yellowstone River.

2. Serengeti National Park: Serengeti National Park is located in Tanzania and is one of the most popular safari destinations in Africa. The park spans over 14,000 square kilometers and is home to a wide range of wildlife, including lions, cheetahs, and zebras. Visitors to Serengeti can take part in guided safaris and witness the annual wildebeest migration,

which is one of the most spectacular natural events in the world.

3. Great Barrier Reef Marine Park: Located off the coast of Australia, the Great Barrier Reef is the largest coral reef system in the world and is home to an incredible array of marine life. The Great Barrier Reef Marine Park spans over 344,000 square kilometers and is home to over 1,500 species of fish, as well as sharks, turtles, and dolphins. Visitors can take part in snorkeling and scuba diving tours to explore the vibrant coral reefs and observe the diverse marine life.

4. Banff National Park: Banff National Park is located in the Canadian Rockies and is known for its stunning mountain landscapes and pristine lakes. The park spans over 6,600 square kilometers and is home to a variety of wildlife, including grizzly bears, elk, and moose. Visitors can take part in a range of activities, such as hiking, skiing, and camping, and visit popular attractions such as Lake Louise and the Banff Hot Springs.

5. Galapagos Islands: Located off the coast of Ecuador, the Galapagos Islands are a group of volcanic islands known for their unique wildlife, including giant tortoises and marine iguanas. The islands are also home to a range of marine life, including sharks, sea lions, and penguins. Visitors to the Galapagos Islands can take part in guided tours to explore the islands' diverse ecosystems and learn about the ongoing conservation efforts to protect the fragile ecosystem.

Conclusion: National parks and nature reserves offer visitors an opportunity to immerse themselves in nature and experience some of the world's most breathtaking landscapes and wildlife. Whether you're looking for a safari adventure or a scenic hike, there's a national park or nature reserve out there that's perfect for you. So, pack your bags, lace up your hiking boots, and get ready for an unforgettable day trip or excursion in the great outdoors.

Historical and cultural sites

Exploring the historical and cultural sites in a destination is a great way to learn about its past and present. Many historical and cultural sites are located just a short distance from popular tourist areas, making them perfect for day trips and excursions. In this section, we will discuss some of the most fascinating and educational historical and cultural sites that you can visit during your travels.

1. Ancient ruins

One of the most popular types of historical sites to visit are ancient ruins. Many countries around the world have ruins from ancient civilizations, such as Greece, Rome, and Egypt. Visiting these ruins can give you a glimpse into the past and help you understand the history and culture of the region. Some of the most famous ancient ruins include the Acropolis in Athens, the Colosseum in Rome, and the pyramids in Egypt.

2. Museums

Museums are also popular destinations for those interested in history and culture. They offer a variety of exhibits that showcase the art, artifacts, and historical events of a region. Many museums also offer guided tours and educational programs for visitors. Some of the most famous museums in the world include the Louvre in Paris, the Smithsonian in Washington D.C., and the British Museum in London.

3. Religious sites

Religious sites, such as churches, mosques, and temples, are also important historical and cultural destinations. They often showcase the architecture, art, and religious practices of a region. Many of these sites are also considered to be sacred and have great significance to the local community. Some of the most famous religious sites in the world include the Vatican in Rome, the Blue Mosque in Istanbul, and the Shinto shrines in Japan.

4. Castles and palaces

Castles and palaces are also popular historical and cultural sites to visit. These grand structures often have a rich history and can showcase the art, architecture, and lifestyle of the wealthy and powerful. Many of these sites offer guided tours and special events for visitors. Some of the most famous castles and palaces include the Palace of Versailles in France, Neuschwanstein Castle in Germany, and the Alhambra in Spain.

5. Historical landmarks

Historical landmarks, such as monuments, statues, and buildings, are also popular historical and cultural sites to visit. They often have great significance to a region and can be a source of pride for the local community. Many of these landmarks are also recognized as UNESCO World Heritage Sites. Some of the most famous historical landmarks include the Eiffel Tower in Paris, the Statue of Liberty in New York, and the Great Wall of China.

6. Living history sites

Living history sites, such as colonial villages and reenactment sites, are a unique way to experience history and culture. They often have costumed actors and interactive exhibits that showcase the daily life and customs of a particular time period. Many of these sites also offer workshops and educational programs for visitors. Some of the most famous living history sites include Colonial Williamsburg in Virginia, the Plimoth Plantation in Massachusetts, and the Viking Museum in Norway.

In conclusion, exploring historical and cultural sites can be an enriching and educational experience during your travels. From ancient ruins to living history sites, there are a variety of destinations to choose from depending on your interests. These sites offer a glimpse into the past and present of a region, and can help you gain a deeper appreciation for its history and culture.

Wineries and vineyards

Wineries and vineyards are popular day trip destinations for wine lovers and tourists alike. Many regions around the world are known for their wine production and offer tours and tastings to visitors. Here are some of the best wineries and vineyards to visit:

1. Napa Valley, California, USA Napa Valley is one of the most famous wine regions in the world, producing some of the best Cabernet Sauvignon and Chardonnay wines. The valley is home to over 400 wineries, many of which offer tours and tastings to visitors. Some popular wineries to visit include Robert Mondavi Winery, Beringer Vineyards, and Domaine Carneros.

2. Bordeaux, France Bordeaux is one of the most renowned wine regions in the world, producing some of the most expensive and highly rated wines. The region is home to over 8,500 wineries, many of which offer tours and tastings to visitors. Some popular wineries to visit include Château Margaux, Château Lafite Rothschild, and Château Mouton Rothschild.

3. Tuscany, Italy Tuscany is known for producing some of the best Chianti and Brunello wines. The region is home to over 700 wineries, many of which are family-owned and offer tours and tastings to visitors. Some popular wineries to visit include Castello di Ama, Castello Banfi, and Antinori.

4. Mendoza, Argentina Mendoza is the largest wine region in Argentina and is known for producing some of the best Malbec wines. The region is home to over 1,500 wineries, many of which offer tours and tastings to visitors. Some popular wineries to visit include Bodega Catena Zapata, Bodega Norton, and Familia Zuccardi.

5. Douro Valley, Portugal The Douro Valley is the oldest wine region in the world, dating back to the 3rd century AD. The region is known for producing Port wine and is home to over 100 wineries, many of which offer tours and tastings to visitors. Some popular wineries to visit include Quinta do Noval, Quinta do Crasto, and Quinta do Vallado.

6. Marlborough, New Zealand Marlborough is the largest wine region in New Zealand and is known for producing some of the best Sauvignon Blanc wines. The region is home to over 100 wineries, many of which offer tours and tastings to visitors. Some popular wineries to visit include Cloudy Bay, Wairau River Wines, and Saint Clair Family Estate.

7. Hunter Valley, Australia Hunter Valley is the oldest wine region in Australia and is known for producing some of the best Shiraz and Semillon wines. The region is home to over 150 wineries, many of which offer tours and tastings to visitors. Some popular wineries to visit include Brokenwood Wines, Tyrell's Wines, and McWilliam's Wines.

When visiting wineries and vineyards, it's important to remember to drink responsibly and never drink and drive.

Many wineries also offer food pairings with their wine tastings, so be sure to try some of the local cuisine as well.

Budgeting and cost-saving tips

Traveling can be expensive, but with proper planning and budgeting, it can be more affordable than you think. In this chapter, we'll explore some tips and tricks to help you save money and stick to your budget while traveling.

1. Plan your trip in advance: By planning your trip in advance, you'll have more time to research and find deals on flights, accommodations, and activities. Many airlines and hotels offer early bird discounts, so booking ahead of time can save you a significant amount of money.

2. Choose your destination wisely: Some destinations are more expensive than others, so consider visiting a less popular location or a city during the off-season. This can result in cheaper flights, accommodations, and activities. Additionally, some countries have a lower cost of living, which can help you stretch your budget further.

3. Use budget-friendly accommodations: Hostels, guesthouses, and Airbnb rentals are often cheaper than hotels, especially if you're traveling solo or with a small group. If you're traveling with a larger group, consider renting a vacation home or apartment, which can save you money on food and other expenses.

4. Cook your own meals: Eating out can be a significant expense when traveling, so consider cooking your own meals using local ingredients from a grocery store or market. This can

not only save you money but also allow you to experience local cuisine and culture.

5. Use public transportation: Taxis and rental cars can be expensive, so consider using public transportation such as buses, trains, or subways to get around. Many cities offer day or week passes that can save you money compared to buying individual tickets.

6. Take advantage of free activities: Many museums, parks, and attractions offer free admission or have a suggested donation. Research what free activities are available in your destination, and plan your itinerary accordingly.

7. Be flexible: Sometimes, unexpected expenses can arise during your trip. By being flexible with your itinerary, you can adjust your plans to accommodate these expenses without breaking your budget.

8. Use travel rewards programs: Many airlines, hotels, and credit cards offer rewards programs that can help you save money on future travel expenses. Research which programs are available and how to maximize your rewards.

9. Shop around for deals: Before booking flights, accommodations, or activities, shop around to find the best deals. Websites like Kayak, Expedia, and Travelocity can help you compare prices across different platforms.

10. Keep track of your expenses: Finally, keep track of your expenses throughout your trip to ensure you're staying

within your budget. This can be as simple as using a spreadsheet or budgeting app to log your expenses each day.

By following these tips and tricks, you can save money and stick to your budget while still having an enjoyable and memorable travel experience.

Traveling can be stressful, but with the help of technology, it can be much easier to plan and organize your trip. In this section, we will explore the best travel apps and websites to use for planning and booking your next adventure.

1. Booking and Accommodation One of the most important aspects of travel is booking your accommodation. Here are some popular booking sites:

- Booking.com: One of the largest travel booking sites, Booking.com offers a wide range of accommodations from hotels and resorts to apartments and vacation rentals. They also offer competitive pricing and a loyalty program.

- Airbnb: A popular option for travelers who want a more local experience, Airbnb offers unique accommodations such as apartments, villas, and even treehouses. They also have a feature for experiences and activities.

- Expedia: Expedia offers not only hotel and flight bookings but also car rentals, activities, and travel packages. They often have exclusive deals and promotions.

- Hotels.com: Similar to Booking.com, Hotels.com offers a range of accommodations, including hotels, resorts, and vacation rentals. They also offer a loyalty program that rewards users with a free night after booking 10 nights.

2. Flights Finding cheap flights can be a challenge, but these websites can help:

- Skyscanner: A popular flight aggregator site, Skyscanner compares prices across various airlines and provides users with the cheapest options. They also have a feature for car rentals and hotel bookings.

- Kayak: Kayak not only compares prices but also offers a feature that predicts whether prices will go up or down in the future. They also have a "hacker fares" option that combines two one-way tickets from different airlines to save money.

- Google Flights: Google Flights allows users to search for flights based on their preferred dates and destination. They also have a feature that shows users the cheapest dates to fly and the cheapest airports to fly into.

3. Transportation Getting around your destination can be challenging, but these apps can help:

- Uber/Lyft: These ride-sharing apps are available in many cities around the world and can be a convenient and cost-effective way to get around. They also offer features such as shared rides and luxury car options.

- Google Maps: Google Maps not only provides users with directions but also shows real-time traffic and public transportation schedules. They also have a feature that allows users to download maps for offline use.

- Rome2rio: Rome2rio allows users to compare different modes of transportation, such as trains, buses, and flights, to find the cheapest and most efficient option.

4. Travel Planning and Organization Finally, these apps can help you plan and organize your trip:

- TripIt: TripIt organizes your travel plans, including flights, hotels, and activities, into one itinerary. It also provides real-time alerts and updates.

- Google Trips: Google Trips provides users with personalized recommendations for things to do and places to eat based on their interests and past searches. It also allows users to download trip information for offline use.

- PackPoint: PackPoint helps users pack by providing a personalized packing list based on their destination, activities, and weather forecast.

In conclusion, these travel apps and websites can make your trip planning and organization much easier and stress-free. Be sure to explore and take advantage of their features to make the most out of your next adventure.

Tourist information centers, also known as visitor information centers, are locations where travelers can get information about a destination and the services available to them. These centers can provide a wide range of services, including maps, brochures, accommodation recommendations, transportation information, and sightseeing advice. In this section, we will explore what tourist information centers are, what services they provide, and how to make the most of them during your travels.

What are Tourist Information Centers? Tourist information centers are physical locations where visitors can find information about a destination. They are typically operated by local or regional tourism boards, government agencies, or private companies. These centers are designed to be a one-stop-shop for travelers, providing a wealth of information and resources in one convenient location. They can be found in airports, train stations, city centers, and other popular tourist areas.

What Services Do Tourist Information Centers Provide? Tourist information centers provide a wide range of services to travelers. These services can include:

1. Information about attractions and events: Tourist information centers can provide information about popular attractions, events, and festivals in the area. This can help

travelers plan their itinerary and make the most of their time in the destination.

2. Maps and brochures: Tourist information centers typically have a variety of maps and brochures available for travelers. These resources can help visitors navigate the destination and learn about local culture and history.

3. Accommodation recommendations: Tourist information centers can provide information about accommodation options in the area. They can recommend hotels, bed and breakfasts, and other types of lodging based on the traveler's budget and preferences.

4. Transportation information: Tourist information centers can provide information about transportation options in the destination. This can include information about public transportation, taxis, and rental cars.

5. Sightseeing advice: Tourist information centers can provide advice about popular sightseeing spots, as well as lesser-known hidden gems. They can recommend tours, activities, and other experiences based on the traveler's interests.

6. Multilingual staff: Tourist information centers often have staff members who speak multiple languages. This can be helpful for international travelers who may have difficulty communicating in the local language.

How to Make the Most of Tourist Information Centers? To make the most of tourist information centers, it's important to plan ahead and know what information you need. Here are some tips for making the most of tourist information centers:

1. Research ahead of time: Before you arrive at your destination, research the tourist information centers in the area. This will help you plan your itinerary and know where to go for information.

2. Ask questions: Don't be afraid to ask questions when you visit a tourist information center. The staff members are there to help you, and they are often locals who know the destination well.

3. Be specific: When asking for information, be as specific as possible. This will help the staff members provide you with the most accurate and helpful information.

4. Take advantage of free resources: Many tourist information centers provide free maps, brochures, and other resources. Take advantage of these resources to help you navigate the destination.

5. Check for discounts: Some tourist information centers offer discounts on attractions, tours, and other experiences. Be sure to ask if there are any discounts available that you can take advantage of.

In conclusion, tourist information centers are valuable resources for travelers. They can provide a wealth of information and resources to help visitors make the most of their time in a destination. By planning ahead, asking questions, and taking advantage of the services available, travelers can make their trips more enjoyable and memorable.

Travel agencies and tour operators

Travel agencies and tour operators play an important role in the travel industry by providing a wide range of services that help travelers plan and book their trips. These services can include everything from flight bookings to hotel reservations, transportation, and tours. In this section, we'll take a closer look at travel agencies and tour operators and the benefits they offer to travelers.

What is a Travel Agency?

A travel agency is a company that specializes in providing travel-related services to clients. These services may include flight bookings, hotel reservations, transportation, and tours. Travel agencies can be independent or part of a larger chain, and they can offer a range of travel-related services or specialize in one area such as adventure travel, luxury travel, or business travel.

Benefits of Using a Travel Agency

Using a travel agency can offer many benefits to travelers, including:

1. Time-saving: Planning a trip can be time-consuming, especially if you're not familiar with the destination. A travel agency can help you save time by handling all the details of your trip, from flights to accommodations and activities.

2. Cost-saving: Travel agencies often have access to exclusive deals and discounts that aren't available to the public.

They can also help you find the best deals on flights, hotels, and tours, helping you save money on your trip.

3. Expert advice: Travel agents are knowledgeable about different destinations and can provide valuable advice on things like the best time to visit, local customs, and must-see attractions. They can also help you plan an itinerary that suits your interests and budget.

4. Personalized service: Travel agents can tailor their services to meet your individual needs and preferences, whether you're traveling solo, with a group, or as a family.

What is a Tour Operator?

A tour operator is a company that specializes in designing and operating tours for travelers. Tour operators create and organize tours that include transportation, accommodations, meals, and activities. They often work with travel agencies to promote their tours to a wider audience.

Benefits of Using a Tour Operator

Using a tour operator can offer many benefits to travelers, including:

1. Convenience: Tour operators take care of all the details of your trip, from transportation to accommodations and activities. This makes traveling more convenient and stress-free.

2. Expertise: Tour operators are experts in the destinations they offer and can provide valuable information and advice on local customs, attractions, and activities.

3. Group travel: Tour operators offer group tours, which can be a great way to meet new people and share the experience of traveling with others.

4. Safety and security: Tour operators take steps to ensure the safety and security of their clients, including providing experienced guides and taking precautions to avoid potential risks.

Choosing a Travel Agency or Tour Operator

When choosing a travel agency or tour operator, it's important to do your research and choose a reputable company with a track record of providing quality services. Look for companies that are licensed and bonded, and read reviews from previous clients to get an idea of their experience.

It's also important to choose a company that specializes in the type of travel you're interested in. If you're looking for adventure travel, for example, look for a company that specializes in adventure tours and has experience in the destinations you're interested in.

In conclusion, travel agencies and tour operators offer valuable services to travelers, helping them save time and money while providing expert advice and personalized service. By choosing a reputable company that specializes in the type of travel you're interested in, you can enjoy a stress-free and memorable travel experience.

Conclusion

Recap of the book's content

Throughout this book, we have explored various aspects of travel, from planning and preparation to outdoor activities and cultural experiences. We have discussed the importance of researching destinations, creating a travel budget, and utilizing resources such as travel apps, websites, and tourist information centers.

In Chapter 2, we delved into the different modes of transportation available to travelers, including air travel, trains, buses, and rental cars. We also provided tips for navigating airports, train stations, and public transportation systems.

Chapter 3 focused on practical travel information, including visa requirements, health and safety tips, and currency exchange. We highlighted the importance of staying safe while traveling and provided suggestions for protecting oneself and belongings.

Chapter 4 explored the rich cultural experiences that travelers can encounter, including festivals and events, performing arts and music, cultural institutions, and local customs and traditions. We discussed the importance of immersing oneself in the local culture and taking part in cultural activities to gain a deeper understanding of the destination.

In Chapter 5, we explored outdoor activities such as hiking, water sports and activities, skiing, and adventure tourism. We provided tips for planning and preparing for outdoor activities and highlighted the benefits of spending time in nature.

Chapter 6 focused on day trips and excursions, including nearby towns and villages, national parks and nature reserves, historical and cultural sites, and wineries and vineyards. We provided suggestions for exploring the surrounding areas and discovering the hidden gems of a destination.

Finally, in Chapter 7, we discussed travel planning and resources, including budgeting and cost-saving tips, travel apps and websites, and travel agencies and tour operators. We provided suggestions for finding the best deals and utilizing resources to plan a memorable and stress-free trip.

Overall, this book has aimed to provide a comprehensive guide to planning and enjoying travel. By following the tips and suggestions outlined in these chapters, readers can feel confident and prepared for their next adventure. Whether it's exploring the cultural sites of a new city or embarking on an adrenaline-pumping adventure, travel offers endless opportunities for growth, exploration, and adventure.

Final travel tips and advice

After reading through this guide and planning your trip, there are still some important tips and advice to keep in mind to ensure a successful and enjoyable travel experience. Here are some final travel tips and advice to consider before embarking on your journey.

1. Stay organized

Keeping track of all your travel documents, reservations, and important information can be overwhelming, but staying organized can save you a lot of stress and headaches. Use a travel planner or app to keep everything in one place and easily accessible.

2. Be flexible

While it's important to have an itinerary and plan in place, it's also important to be flexible and adaptable to changes. Weather, transportation delays, and unexpected events can happen, so having a backup plan or being open to changing your plans can help you make the most of your trip.

3. Stay safe

Safety should always be a top priority when traveling. Research the destination's safety concerns and take necessary precautions such as carrying a copy of your passport and keeping valuables secure. Also, be aware of your surroundings and trust your instincts.

4. Respect local customs and culture

When traveling to a new place, it's important to respect and appreciate the local customs and culture. Take the time to learn about the local customs and dress appropriately. Be respectful when visiting religious or cultural sites and avoid any behaviors that may be considered offensive or disrespectful.

5. Try local cuisine

One of the best ways to experience a new culture is through its food. Be adventurous and try new dishes and local specialties. Ask locals for recommendations on where to eat and what to try.

6. Pack smart

Packing can be a challenge, but packing smart can make your trip much easier. Pack versatile and comfortable clothing and only bring essentials. Consider packing a small bag or daypack for day trips and excursions.

7. Stay connected

Staying connected with friends and family back home can help ease any homesickness and keep loved ones updated on your trip. Consider purchasing a local SIM card or using a travel app to stay connected while on the go.

8. Take care of yourself

Traveling can be exhausting, so it's important to take care of yourself. Stay hydrated, get enough sleep, and take breaks when needed. Don't overdo it and take time to relax and enjoy the experience.

In conclusion, traveling can be an incredible and life-changing experience. With proper planning, research, and a willingness to be flexible and adaptable, your trip can be a success. Follow these final travel tips and advice to make the most of your journey and create memories that will last a lifetime.

Call to action for readers to visit the featured capital cities

As we come to the end of this book, I hope that you have found the information helpful and inspiring. Throughout the pages, we have explored some of the world's most fascinating capital cities and all that they have to offer. From rich cultural experiences to outdoor adventures, we have delved into the heart of each city and discovered its unique charm and allure.

Now, I'd like to take a moment to encourage you to take the next step in your travel journey and plan a trip to one of the featured capital cities. Whether you have a specific destination in mind or are open to exploring new possibilities, the world is full of incredible places waiting to be discovered.

Before you pack your bags and set off on your adventure, I want to offer some final travel tips and advice to help make your trip a success.

First and foremost, make sure to do your research before you go. This includes learning about the local culture and customs, as well as any practical information such as currency exchange rates and transportation options. By doing your homework ahead of time, you can avoid any unnecessary stress or confusion once you arrive.

Secondly, be flexible and open to new experiences. Traveling is all about exploring new cultures and stepping outside of your comfort zone. Embrace the unexpected and don't be afraid to try new things.

Another important tip is to pack light and bring only the essentials. Not only will this make it easier to navigate airports and public transportation, but it will also give you more flexibility in terms of where you can go and what you can do.

Lastly, be respectful of the local environment and the people who call it home. Remember that you are a guest in their country and it's important to act accordingly. This means following local customs and traditions, being mindful of your impact on the environment, and treating locals with kindness and respect.

In conclusion, the world is full of incredible capital cities just waiting to be explored. By taking the time to plan and prepare for your trip, staying open to new experiences, and being respectful of the local culture and environment, you can make the most of your travels and create memories that will last a lifetime. So, what are you waiting for? Start planning your next adventure today!

THE END

Key Terms and Definitions

To help you better understand the language and concepts related to aging and older adults, below you will find a list of key terms and their definitions.

1. Travel: The act of moving from one place to another for business, leisure or other reasons.

2. Tourism: The industry that involves traveling to different places for leisure, business or other purposes.

3. Capital city: A city that serves as the administrative center of a country or region.

4. Culture: The customs, arts, social institutions, and achievements of a particular nation, people, or other social group.

5. Heritage: The cultural, historical, and natural resources that are inherited from past generations.

6. Landmarks: A prominent or well-known feature of a landscape or cityscape, typically one of historical or cultural significance.

7. Outdoor activities: Activities that take place in the open air, such as hiking, skiing, and water sports.

8. Adventure tourism: Tourism that involves outdoor activities and/or adventure sports such as bungee jumping, rafting, and zip-lining.

9. Accommodation: A place to stay, such as a hotel, hostel, or vacation rental.

10. Tourist information center: A facility that provides information and advice to tourists, such as maps, brochures, and recommendations for local attractions and activities.

Introduction

No references necessary

Chapter 1: Must-See Attractions

- Lonely Planet. (2021). Top 10 countries to visit in 2021.

https://www.lonelyplanet.com/articles/best-countries-to-visit

- UNESCO. (n.d.). World Heritage List.

https://whc.unesco.org/en/list/

Chapter 2: Hidden Gems

- Atlas Obscura. (n.d.). Discover hidden wonders.

https://www.atlasobscura.com/

- Off the Beaten Path. (n.d.). Travel inspiration.

https://www.offthebeatenpath.com/travel-inspiration/

Chapter 3: Practical Travel Information

- Centers for Disease Control and Prevention. (2021). COVID-19 travel recommendations by destination.

https://www.cdc.gov/coronavirus/2019-ncov/travelers/map-and-travel-notices.html

- U.S. Department of State. (2021). Smart Traveler Enrollment Program. https://step.state.gov/

Chapter 4: Cultural Experiences

- National Geographic. (n.d.). Cultural experiences.

https://www.nationalgeographic.com/travel/experiences/cultural-experiences/

- UNESCO. (n.d.). Intangible Cultural Heritage.

https://ich.unesco.org/en/home

Chapter 5: Outdoor Activities

- American Hiking Society. (n.d.). Hiking resources. https://americanhiking.org/resources/

- International Ski Federation. (n.d.). About skiing. https://www.fis-ski.com/en/skiing

Chapter 6: Day Trips and Excursions

- National Park Service. (n.d.). Find a park. https://www.nps.gov/findapark/index.htm

- TripAdvisor. (n.d.). Things to do. https://www.tripadvisor.com/Attractions

Chapter 7: Travel Planning and Resources

- Kayak. (n.d.). Flights. https://www.kayak.com/flights

- Skyscanner. (n.d.). Cheap flights. https://www.skyscanner.com/tips-and-inspiration/cheap-flights

Conclusion: No references necessary.